Y 2 K

Y 2 K

Arthur Kopit

THE OVERLOOK PRESS
WOODSTOCK & NEW YORK

First published in the United States in 2000 by
The Overlook Press, Peter Mayer Publishers, Inc.
Lewis Hollow Road
Woodstock, New York 12498
www.overlookpress.com

Cataloging-in-Publication Data is available from the Library of Congress

Book design and type formatting by Bernard Schleifer
Manufactured in the United States of America
FIRST EDITION
1 3 5 7 9 8 6 4 2
ISBN 1-58567-025-1

FOR ALEX, BEN, AND KAT

CAST

Costa Astrakhan (a.k.a. BCuzICan, FlowBare, and ISeeU)
Joseph Elliot (early 50s)
Joanne Summerhays Elliot (late 30s)
Orin Slake (looks to be in his 40s)
Dennis McAlvane (a bit younger than Slake)

Time: the summer before the turn of the century.
The play is to be performed without an intermission

Y2K had its world premiere in the 1999 Humana Festival of New American Plays at Actors Theatre of Louisville in February 1999. It was directed by Bob Balaban with the following cast:

Costa Astrakhan (a.k.a. *BCuzICan*, *FlowBare*, and *ISeeU*)

	Dallas Roberts
Joseph Elliot	Graeme Malcolm
Orin Slake	Fred Major
Dennis McAlvane	Thomas Lyons
Joanne Summerhays Elliot	Lucinda Faraldo

and the following production staff:

Scenic Designer	Paul Owen
Costume Designer	Nanzi J. Adzima
Lighting Designer	Pip Gordon
Sound Designer	Malcolm Nicholls
Properties Designer	Ben Hohman
Stage Manager	Charles M. Turner III
Production Assistant	Amber D. Martin
Dramaturg	Michael Bigelow Dixon
Assistant Dramaturg	Sara Skolnick
Casting	Laura Richin Casting

The New York premiere of *Y2K* was produced by the Manhattan Theatre Club on November 9, 1999 at the Lucille Lortel Theatre. It was directed by Bob Balaban with the following cast:

Costa Astrakhan (a.k.a. *BCuzICan*, *FlowBare*, and *ISeeU*)

	Erik Jensen
Joseph Elliot	James Naughton
Orin Slake	Armand Schultz
Dennis McAlvane	David Brown Jr.
Joanne Summerhays Elliot	Patricia Kalember

and the following production staff:

Set Design	Loy Arcenas
Costume Design	Tom Broecker
Lighting Design	Kevin Adams
Sound Design	Darron L. West
Production Stage Manager	James Fitzsimmons

PREFACE

The idea for this play came so swiftly it caught me by surprise. The motor that began it all was outrage.

The outrage I felt was directed at the way Kenneth Starr was pursuing Monica Lewinsky. It was a feeling that grew stronger by the day. And then it became alarm.

Not that Starr had misjudged the situation. Obviously, Lewinsky and the President had had sex, and obviously Clinton had lied about it—as I think surely any man would under those circumstances. To me, it was beyond dispute: What Clinton had done was wholly inappropriate, but the action being taken against him was even more so. These were not nuclear secrets he had given away. The threat his actions posed to our country was minimal. Which is not to suggest he didn't deserve censure. Presidents are not supposed to do that sort of thing in the Oval Office.

But the outrage I was feeling went completely off the charts when Starr tried to subpoena records showing what books Monica Lewinsky had bought. I thought, my God, there's no stopping him! This is fascism! I meant it. No exaggeration. If you're looking for a threat to our country, *this* is where it is.

And that's when my outrage turned into alarm. And it was that sense of alarm that led me to thinking about the ways all of us were vulnerable to such an assault—in the future, and right now. And those thoughts are what led to this play.

I immediately knew the one thing I would *not* write about was Clinton and Starr. What had caught hold of me was an aspect of that situation, and I wanted to explore that single aspect, nothing else.

Ideas came rapidly, with a structure falling into place almost at once—in fact, well before I knew what my story was.

Here was what I saw: that on some fundamental level, the play would be erotic, voyeuristic, and illicit; that technology was key, because the new technology allows people with the proper know-how to gain access to just about anyone's *supposedly* private domain; and that something terrible would happen, for no apparent reason, to a couple, a likeable couple, no better or worse than anybody else, and it would hit so rapidly they'd have hardly any time to get ready, or understand what it was that was occurring until it was over, and too late.

I was in an earthquake once, in Mexico, and it's startling how, in an instant, what you've always believed to be solid turns out not to be. I mean the ground. One moment it's as firm as it's always been, and a moment later, it's as if you're standing on a waterbed. It's just *rippling*. And then you hear them—dogs, howling everywhere. They don't like it either. Ground is not supposed to behave this way.

And all at once, emotionally, you have a totally new view of what real solidity means, and what it doesn't mean. And you're not sure anymore if it even exists.

That idea is at the heart of the movement of this play.

And I saw that what I wanted to do with this play—even before I knew the actual story—was take the audience's breath away the way mine had been taken away that night in Mexico, when, without warning, solid became fluid.

And that's why my play doesn't so much end as stop. It's about the suddenness of it all.

—ARTHUR KOPIT
September, 1999

"To choose one's victims, to prepare one's plan minutely, to slake an implacable vengeance, and then to go to bed ... there is nothing sweeter in the world."

—JOSEF STALIN

(*A narrow spot of light illumines* COSTA ASTRAKHAN (*a.k.a.
BCuzICan, FlowBare, and ISeeU*), *taking us all in through
almond-shaped sunglasses.*

ASTRAKHAN *is 19, but one might not guess it, for he looks so
wasted and haunted that were we told he was in his middle
twenties, we wouldn't be surprised.*

*His hair is neon blue; his shoes, suede and electric green.
He wears black leather pants and leather coat, ala Mel
Gibson in* Road Warrior. *Under his jacket is a T-shirt that
says "Nemesis."*)

ASTRAKHAN

Though you think you see me now, I promise you, you do not. It is
not possible. In fact, I am everywhere—on the outskirts of your
mind, in the ether, in the darkness. And when I'm on the hunt, as
relentless as the wrath of God.

(*Lights Up on:*
THREE MEN *standing in a room lit by one bare dangling
bulb. Under the bulb is a solitary chair.*

Across from the chair is a table with two chairs behind it.

*Of the three men, one seems confused by where he is. His
name is* JOSEPH ELLIOT, *he's in his early 50s, and wears a*

casual but elegant tweed jacket and well-pressed jeans.

The two men with him, ORIN SLAKE *and* DENNIS MCALVANE, *wear the kinds of dark, undistinguished suits, white shirts, and ties favored by the Secret Service.*

SLAKE, *in his forties, has an open, friendly face and an easy smile.* MCALVANE, *being younger, and still a trainee, tries to emulate Slake.*

JOSEPH *looks around in surprise.*)

SLAKE
I imagine, right now, you are wondering why we have brought you here and not to our office. Tell him.

MCALVANE
Bringing you to our office would only attract attention.

SLAKE
To *you*. And who wants that?

MCALVANE
Rumors, you know. Hard to stop 'em once they start!

SLAKE
I'm sorry: can we get you something?

JOSEPH
Yes. A phone. So I can call my lawyer.

(SLAKE *hands him a cell phone.*)

SLAKE
There is really no need, you know.
  (JOSEPH *starts to dial.*)
We just want to ask you a few questions.

MCALVANE
You can leave any time you wish. Really.

JOSEPH

(into phone)
Dotty, hi, it's Joe Elliot, is Larry in by any chance?

SLAKE

We mean that.

JOSEPH

Well when do you expect him?

SLAKE

Any time at all.

JOSEPH

Well when he calls, tell him I've been picked up by two Federal Agents—yes, dear, Federal Agents—who've brought me to a room in a warehouse in Soho George Orwell would feel happy in.

SLAKE

If you prefer, we can do this in a restaurant.

JOSEPH

No, no, this is fun, I'm enjoying this.
(into phone)
Yes, that's right, Federal Agents. They showed me a badge.
(to SLAKE and MCALVANE)
What are your names?

SLAKE

It doesn't matter.

JOSEPH

(into phone)
Did you hear what he just said?
(to SLAKE and MCALVANE)
Larry will be pleased with that!
(into the phone)
Anyhow, tell Larry if I'm never heard from again, this is a clue.
(to SLAKE, re the cell phone)
Can Larry call me back on this?

SLAKE

No.

JOSEPH

(into the phone)

From this moment forward, it seems I am in the hands of the gods.

(He clicks off; hands back the phone.)

I'm curious. What would you have done if I'd say no, sorry, fuck off, I am not going anywhere with you. Would you have let me continue on my way?

SLAKE

Of course.

JOSEPH

Really!

SLAKE

As I said, you're just doing us a courtesy.

JOSEPH

Then you should know I have a luncheon in one hour.

SLAKE

Yes, at the Gramercy Tavern, we know. I'm sure we'll be done by then.

(JOSEPH stares at SLAKE, startled.)

MCALVANE

Would you like to sit?

(MCALVANE gestures to the solitary chair under the light— not the sort of place one would choose, given a choice.)

JOSEPH

Could I sit over there instead?

MCALVANE

We'd prefer if you sat here.

JOSEPH

Why don't we just all sit together!

SLAKE

Fine. Mac?

MCALVANE

Coming up!

> (MCALVANE *carries the two other chairs toward the one in the middle. They sit.*)

JOSEPH

So what is it you want to know?

SLAKE

Does the name Feted mean anything to you?

JOSEPH

. . . *Name?*

SLAKE

Yes.

JOSEPH

You sure you don't mean "word"?

SLAKE

No.

MCALVANE

Name.

JOSEPH

First or last?

SLAKE

It's an alias.

JOSEPH

"Fetid."

McALVANE

Yes.

JOSEPH

As in—

McALVANE

Wined and dined.

JOSEPH

Ah! No. Means nothing.

SLAKE

What about—
(opens a notepad; reads)
ShortCurlies, BungHole, or ISeeU.

JOSEPH

I'm sorry, but are you aware how odd these questions are?

McALVANE

Very.

JOSEPH

Well that's encouraging! So. ICU—as in "Intensive Care Unit"?
Or—

SLAKE

(miming it as he speaks)
I see you.

JOSEPH

I see. To the best of my knowledge, I have never met or conversed
with anyone who refers to himself as I-See-You.

SLAKE

What about corresponded?

JOSEPH

Nor corresponded.

MCALVANE

Are you sure?

JOSEPH

Is that another name?

MCALVANE

No, a question.

SLAKE

Have you ever received anything—

MCALVANE

—by either hand or mail—

SLAKE

—from a man who calls himself ISeeU.

JOSEPH

Not that I recall.

MCALVANE

Which means you may have.

JOSEPH

Only if he called himself something else. I say that with trepidation, knowing it opens the door to almost limitless possibilities. He could for example be one of our authors.

SLAKE

That's what I was going to ask next.

JOSEPH

To my knowledge, not one Random House author, and I am includ-
ing there both current and backlist, has ever used the name I-See-
You.

McALVANE

What about BungHole?

JOSEPH

Now there I'm not so sure.
  (They look at him with suspicion.)
I'm joking! I mean—All right, the truth: on several occasions I have
heard people in my office, generally in the heat of argument, say,
"You bunghole!" Were they in fact saying, "You comma Bunghole?"
—of that I am not sure.

SLAKE

What about your wife?

JOSEPH

My wife, to my knowledge, has never uttered the word "bunghole"
in her life. But then, I've only known her since she was twenty-
eight—no, sorry, twenty-seven. Who can say how her youth was
spent?

SLAKE

Exactly. In such matters, who can really say?

McALVANE

Is it possible that *she* is acquainted with ISeeU?

JOSEPH

I wouldn't think so.

SLAKE

How can you be certain?

JOSEPH

I am certain because if she *were* acquainted with someone named
I-See-You I assure you she'd have told me by now.

SLAKE

He knows *her.*

JOSEPH

Well he's LYING!

(They stare at him.

Beat.

Lights out

Lights back on ASTRAKHAN.)

ASTRAKHAN

And though you cannot see where I really am, I can see all of you. In fact, can see any part of you I wish—your cunts, your bank accounts, your charge accounts. Is that fair? Not at all. That's just how it is. I'm being honest now. Which is not to say that usually I'm not. Because I am. Usually. I mean honest. Honest as the day is long. So when I tell you that you cannot hide from me so don't even try, you should fucking well take my word for it.

(Lights up on:
JOSEPH'S *Park Avenue apartment,* JOSEPH, *dressed as before, staring at his wife,* JOANNE, *late 30s, dressed in a simple, understatedly elegant suit.)*

JOSEPH
(finally)
I'm sorry; you don't find this . . . "odd"?
(She turns and looks at him; no idea what he's talking about.)
What I've been telling you.
(Still a blank.)
For the past hour.
(That notion startles her.)
All right, twenty minutes.

JOANNE

Give me a hint.

JOSEPH
Two Federal agents. A warehouse down in Soho.

JOANNE
You'd think that would be enough.

JOSEPH
Wouldn't you?

JOANNE
I'm sorry, Joseph, this has not been a good day for me. Would you like a drink?

JOSEPH
Sure.

JOANNE
Vodka and tonic?

JOSEPH
Vodka and vodka.
    (*She exits.*)
By the way, did Larry call?

JOANNE (*Offstage*)
No. Only Emma.

JOSEPH
Emma?

JOANNE (*Offstage*)
She's in Paris.

JOSEPH
What's she doing there?

JOANNE (*Offstage*)
Didn't say.

JOSEPH

Well why didn't you ask?

JOANNE (*Offstage*)

It was on the machine.

JOSEPH

Ah.

JOANNE (*Offstage*)

Do you want vermouth?

JOSEPH

No. Not even ice. So wha'd she say?

JOANNE (*Offstage*)

That she received an obscene phone call this morning.

JOSEPH

In Paris?

JOANNE: (*Offstage*)

Obviously! That's where she is.

JOSEPH

And she called from Paris just to say that?

JOANNE: (*Offstage*)

No, she called to say that the man who phoned her . . .
   (*pokes her head back in*)
. . . sounded exactly like you.

JOSEPH

Jesus.

JOANNE

She thought you'd be interested. Any idea where I might find the corkscrew?

JOSEPH
You don't need the corkscrew for vodka.

JOANNE
I've decided to have wine.

JOSEPH
Ah. No. No idea.
(She disappears again.)
Did she say what hotel she was in?

JOANNE *(Offstage)*
No. Sorry.

JOSEPH
Right.

JOANNE *(Offstage)*
She said it was a very disturbing call.

JOSEPH
. . . Yes . . . I'm sure . . .

(He stares out, puzzled and vaguely troubled.

Lights back on ASTRAKHAN. *)*

ASTRAKHAN
My original mentor was the group known as MoD—that's capital
M, small o, Capital D—and stands for Masters of Downloading,
a rowdy bunch, quick with the quip and by and large I would say
fearless, but I quickly moved away from them into a hitherto
unknown region of digital hyperspace that was, to be blunt,
beyond their imagining.

Yet I am a gracious soul, and left them a farewell gift—a
password cracker I call Willie Sutton. This little gem, currently
available at www.nemesis.com will defeat UNIX, DOS, Windows95,
98, NT and is compatible with Linux x86/ Alpha/SPARC/
FreeBSD86 and OpenBSD. Even more astonishing, out of the box,
Willie Sutton supports standard and double-length DES-based

and OpenBSD's Blowfish-based ciphertext! If you have understood nothing of what I have just said, don't go near this stuff. It could only do you in.

A hint: learn it. With what I know, I can go anywhere, and you can too. I have done the math. Do you have the courage?

(*Lights off on* ASTRAKHAN *and back up on* JOSEPH *as* JOANNE *enters carrying vodka and wine on a tray*)

JOANNE

So, two Federal Agents . . .

JOSEPH

(*going for the vodka*)
Interrogated me in a seemingly abandoned warehouse somewhere in Soho for about an hour and a half.

JOANNE

What?

JOSEPH

An appropriate reaction!

JOANNE

Joseph . . .

JOSEPH

But do not fret. As I left, they said they were sure it was probably all a mistake.

JOANNE

Mistake?

JOSEPH

I think they meant of identity, but I'm not certain.

JOANNE

Did they say anything about obscene phone calls to Paris?

JOSEPH

This is not funny!

JOANNE

Sorry.
   (*She sips some wine.*)
Well you should call Larry.

JOSEPH

I did, but he hasn't called back.

JOANNE

Are you worried?

JOSEPH

No. No, he'll call.

JOANNE

I mean about the Feds.

JOSEPH

Do I *look* worried?

JOANNE

No, but I can't always tell with you.

JOSEPH

Well I am not worried, I am fucking PISSED OFF!

JOANNE

That seems like a very healthy attitude. Cheers!

JOSEPH

It's outrageous!

JOANNE

To a *warehouse?*

JOSEPH

"So as not to attract *attention*."

JOANNE

You're not serious.

JOSEPH

It's what they said. Place smelled of dead meat. Oh, guess who was in with Perry.

JOANNE

Perry?

JOSEPH

When I got back to the office.

JOANNE

. . . Give up.

JOSEPH

Tom Clancy.

JOANNE

I thought he was with Putnam.

JOSEPH

He is, but Perry was all smiles so I think something may be up. Anyway, I gave them a brief account of my morning's adventures, and they both agreed they had never heard of such a thing, but that if I played it right it could lead to all sorts of wonderful dinner invitations. You can even come along!

JOANNE

Are you sure you're not in trouble?

JOSEPH

No, I am not sure, not at all. Anyway, that was *my* day. How was yours? Terrible, I know. Tell me.

JOANNE

Compared to yours, it was nothing.

JOSEPH

To compare *anyone's* with mine is unfair. This is not a competition.
What happened to you?

JOANNE

Francis called.

JOSEPH

Oh God . . .

JOANNE

I can't stop him from calling me.

JOSEPH

What about a restraining order?

JOANNE

Joseph, be sensible.

JOSEPH

Well certainly you don't have to *take* the call.

JOANNE

Francis is nothing if not persistent.

JOSEPH

That doesn't mean you have to take the call!

JOANNE

If you're going to shout—

JOSEPH

I am not shouting!
    (*softer*)
Not shouting.

JOANNE

I took the call because he'd been phoning every fifteen minutes for two days straight, and Stephanie was getting tired of telling him I wasn't in.

JOSEPH

What about telling him you *are* in but prefer not to take his call, today, tomorrow, and forever more.

JOANNE

We tried that.

JOSEPH

And?

JOANNE

He started faxing me and it tied up the line. The fax machine is a significant tool at Sotheby's.

JOSEPH

So you spoke to him.

JOANNE

Yes. I spoke to him.

JOSEPH

And I trust told him to fuck off.

JOANNE

That sort of approach only inspires him.

JOSEPH

So what did he want?

JOANNE

I think it may be time to switch to vodka.

JOSEPH

What did he want, Joanne?

JOANNE

What do you think?

JOSEPH

It is nice, I must say, to have someone in your life you despise so intensely that you need only conjure up his name when you are bored to get an instant rush of adrenaline. Sometimes I think I could kill him.

JOANNE

No you can't; he's already dead. Read Anne Rice.

JOSEPH

I meant a stake through the heart.

JOANNE

Ah.

JOSEPH

So what did dear Francis say?

JOANNE

The usual.

JOSEPH

Jesus!

JOANNE

Complete with anatomical details. I said. "That's nice, Francis, keep dreaming," and hung up.

JOSEPH

Does he think you get some kind of charge from this?

JOANNE

I'm afraid to say, I've never actually inquired.

JOSEPH

Do you?

JOANNE

Think he gets a charge?

JOSEPH

Get one.

JOANNE

Yes, I get all wet. You should see my legs, right now, dripping, just from this.

JOSEPH

Joanne—

JOANNE

No, I do not get a charge.

JOSEPH

Even in a creepy sort of way?

JOANNE

Oh my God . . .

JOSEPH

What, you don't think it's possible?

JOANNE

Joseph, darling, making lampshades out of human skin is possible. Does it follow therefore that you'd like to see how it's done?

JOSEPH

I might.

JOANNE

You *might*?

JOSEPH

In the abstract.

JOANNE

Doesn't sound very abstract.

JOSEPH
But if it were, if it somehow *could* be, you know, *presented* . . .

JOANNE
Tastefully.

JOSEPH
Kind of hard to imagine.

JOANNE
Still . . .

(*She pours herself another drink.*)

JOSEPH
Anyway, in this spirit of abstract, unfettered inquiry—

JOANNE
You were wondering if I get any sort of rush when Francis calls to
ask how my pussy's doing.

JOSEPH
Yes.

JOANNE
The answer's no. I am in fact revolted. Is that clear enough?

JOSEPH
Yes.

JOANNE
Are you disappointed?

JOSEPH
No.

JOANNE
Pleased?

JOSEPH

Neither pleased I'd say *nor* disappointed.

JOANNE

What about "surprised"?

JOSEPH

A bit.

JOANNE

Sometimes, I have to tell you, I am really staggered at how little you seem to understand me.

JOSEPH

Actually, I don't think I understand you at all.

JOANNE

Well that's comforting!

JOSEPH

No—no, please, it's exciting.

JOANNE

Part of the adventure!

JOSEPH

Yes.

JOANNE

I can see that, yes, waking up each morning, a blank slate with tits lying next to you in bed.

JOSEPH

Not *quite* what I had in mind.

JOANNE

Good. I've made an impact then.

JOSEPH

So is that it?

JOANNE

What?

JOSEPH

Francis called you up and that was it?

JOANNE

If that were it, I would not be on my second or is it third glass of vodka now.

JOSEPH

So . . . ?

JOANNE

When I left, he was waiting by the curb.

JOSEPH

For you?

JOANNE

Yes, Joseph, for me, big black umbrella in his fucking hand, limo double-parked, back door open. "Hi, it's raining, thought I'd give you a lift home."

JOSEPH

Tell me you didn't get in.

JOANNE

I did not get in.

JOSEPH

Well thank God for that.

JOANNE

Think I could use another drink.

JOSEPH
Well did you get in his fucking limousine or not?

JOANNE
I got in.

JOSEPH
Well then why did you say you didn't?

JOANNE
Because that is what you asked me to say, and so naturally I assumed it was what you wanted to hear. You've had a rough day, too, and I am trying to be a helpmate.

JOSEPH
So you got in.

JOANNE
It was pouring out.

JOSEPH
Then take a fucking cab!

JOANNE
There weren't any.

JOSEPH
This is really wonderful.

JOANNE
So he drove me home.

JOSEPH
Took the long route, I'm sure.

JOANNE
With all the traffic, going straight was long enough.

JOSEPH

I can't believe you got in his fucking car!

JOANNE

If it makes you feel any better, I can't believe it either.

JOSEPH

What did he do to you?

JOANNE

In the car?

JOSEPH

Yes!

JOANNE

Nothing.

JOSEPH

Well I don't believe it.

JOANNE

All right, fine, he fucked me.

JOSEPH

Jesus!

JOANNE

First on the back seat, then on the floor. He did *nothing* to me, Joseph, not a *thing*! He was a gentleman.

JOSEPH

Francis Summerhays?

JOANNE

Yes, Joseph. When he wants, Francis can be a perfect gentleman.

JOSEPH

"Perfect gentleman!"

JOANNE

Mostly, he asked after you.

JOSEPH

Fuck him!

JOANNE

And I told him not a thing.

JOSEPH

What does *that* mean?

JOANNE

It means I refused to speak about you in any way.

JOSEPH

Why?

JOANNE

Because I didn't want to sully you.

JOSEPH

"Sully"?

JOANNE

Francis has this ability of turning any remark into something unto-ward. I was not pleased to find myself in his car, and I thought the least I can do is keep you out of it.

JOSEPH

Did he touch you?

JOANNE

On my arm, guiding me in, and that was all.

JOSEPH

Hard to believe.

JOANNE

Believe it.

JOSEPH

So then what did you talk about, if all he wanted was to inquire after me?

JOANNE

Nothing.

JOSEPH

Nothing?

JOANNE

Nothing! I was silent the whole way home. And eventually, he shut up too.

JOSEPH

So *then* what did he do?

JOANNE

What do you mean?

JOSEPH

If he is silent in the back, how was he occupying his time? With what endeavor was he filling his fucking time?

JOANNE

(*barely audible*)
. . . He was watching me.

JOSEPH

Watching you.

JOANNE

Yes.

JOSEPH

And what are you doing during this?

JOANNE

Staring out the window.

JOSEPH

So then how did you know?

JOANNE

I could see his reflection.

JOSEPH

Watching you.

JOANNE

Yes. And there you are, there you have it. Would you like another drink?

JOSEPH

No.

JOANNE

Look, I'm sorry. I should not have gotten in. And I've no idea why I did, I just did. Next time, I will be prepared.

(*She pours herself another drink.*

Pause.)

JOSEPH

The men who questioned me asked if I knew anyone who uses the name "I-See-You" as an alias. I said I didn't. They said, well he knows your wife.

JOANNE

If you're thinking that it might be Francis, I can assure you it is not.

JOSEPH

How can you be certain?

JOANNE

Because Francis does not like playing games. It's not his "style." When Francis wants a thing, he goes straight for it. It's his only honest trait.

JOSEPH

Then why did you marry him?

JOANNE

Joseph . . .

JOSEPH

Why?

JOANNE

We've been *through* all this. It does no good.

JOSEPH

Are you still in love with him?

JOANNE

Are you serious?

JOSEPH

Yes.

JOANNE

Then lighten up.

JOSEPH

You got into a car with a man you swear you despise!

JOANNE

It was raining out!

JOSEPH

Is *that* all it takes?

JOANNE

Apparently, some days yes!
(*She pours herself another drink.*)
. . . Then again, some days no. With me, it's hard to say in advance.

JOSEPH

I am trying to get a grip on this!

JOANNE

I've been trying that for years. It's slipp'ry stuff.

JOSEPH

Jesus . . .

JOANNE

One of these days, your blasphemy is going to catch up with you,
Joseph. And the earth is going to open. Watch.

(*She starts to leave.*)

JOSEPH

Joanne!

JOANNE

(*stops; defiant*)
I married him because I thought I loved him, and believed he
would be my rock. On both counts I was wrong. *You* are my rock,
and the only man I've ever truly loved. Why? I've no idea. Life is
fun, isn't it?

(*She leaves. He stares after her, shaken. She comes right
back.*)

I'm sorry, I didn't handle that quite right. Let's try that again. Even
at moments such as this, Joseph, you are who I love, and the only
one I've *ever* loved. And my rock, my one true rock, to whom I am
most profoundly tethered, and in whose lee I am sheltered from all
storms. *That felt a little better.*

JOSEPH

(genuinely moved)
Thank you.

JOANNE

Proves it can be done!

JOSEPH

Yes. Proves it can be done.

(She smiles. The light dims. She moves toward him. He takes her in his arms.

Lights back on ASTRAKHAN, staring out, blank and pitiless.)

ASTRAKHAN

(flat; expressionless)
Joanne Summerhays, born Joanne Elizabeth Simpson, October fifth nineteen sixty-one in Ann Arbor, Michigan, where her father taught moral philosophy at the University and her mother taught the flute.

(In the shadows, JOSEPH slowly begins to remove JOANNE's blouse.

ASTRAKHAN continues to stare out.)

In 1983 Joanne graduates from Princeton with a summa in Art History, and the next fall accepts a position at Sotheby's as an administrative assistant specializing in jade and Chinese porcelain.

Two months later, she meets Francis Summerhays, a venture capitalist, at an auction of Asian art at which Summerhays pays three hundred thousand dollars for two matching porcelain tea cups of the Sung dynasty, whose luster, he tells Joanne, pales in comparison to the luster of her skin. Three months later, she marries him.

(JOSEPH stares at JOANNE in awe.)

But the marriage does not go well, and before the year is out she seeks a divorce—this, according to a journal she starts to keep on her lawyer's advice, first in a notebook, then, later, on her computer at Sotheby's believing it's "more secure."

(JOSEPH *kisses* JOANNE.)

Then, one night, with Francis out of town, Joanne goes to a dinner party where she meets Joseph Elliot, an editor at Random House.

(JOANNE *and* JOSEPH *move to the couch.*)

The next morning she calls her host, ostensibly to thank her for the lovely evening but in fact to inquire about Joe Elliot, whom Joanne had found, quote: "a delightful dinner partner; most intriguing."

Which is when she learns that Joseph is married—to a fragile beauty named Annabel. When Joanne asks what Annabel does, she is told: Annabel is dying of cancer.

Undeterred, Joanne calls Joseph at his office with an idea for a book about Chinese jade which Joseph finds so fascinating he invites her to lunch, where he offers her a book deal. For the next year, their relationship is business-like.

Then, on August the fourth, with Annabel at New York Hospital recovering from yet another round of chemotherapy, Joseph and Joanne become lovers, the event occurring at approximately eleven P.M. on the soft leather Chesterfield couch in Joanne's office.

(JOANNE *and* JOSEPH *decide the bedroom is better for this, and exit.*)

Apparently, remorse almost instantly overcomes them both, and they decide, while still on the couch, to refrain from any further screwing until Annabel is gone for good—which turns out to take far longer than her doctors had predicted.

But, eventually, it does occur. And three months later, recently widowed Joseph Elliot and recently divorced Joanne Summerhays marry in a ceremony which Joseph and Annabel's twelve-year-old daughter, named Emma, refuses to attend. Four years after that, I enter the picture. Which is to say, that is when I first see Joanne. Joseph is my way in. No, let's be honest: to me he is far more than that. In fact, always has been. I just hadn't discovered it yet.

(Lights to black on ASTRAKHAN *and up on:*

JOSEPH's *office at Random House. It is late afternoon, and* JOSEPH *is at his desk,* SLAKE *and* MCALVANE *standing just inside the door, staring at him.*

MCALVANE *carries a slim leather pouch.*

During the course of this scene, the afternoon light fades imperceptibly until, near the end, it becomes so dark that JOSEPH *has to turn on a desk-lamp. But the lamp sheds little light.*

At the start, JOSEPH, *in contrast to the last time these three met, seems at ease.* JOSEPH *believes he is in charge)*

JOSEPH
(rising from behind the desk—cheerfully)
Come in, come in. Sorry. Did I keep you waiting?

SLAKE

Not at all.

JOSEPH
Oh good! The other day—well I've just never *had* an experience like that! Nor, actually, has anyone else I know. So when you called to ask if we could meet again—and this time *here!*—well I was over-joyed! As was the rest of Random House.
(sotto voce, gesturing out toward his workers)
Half of them didn't believe you were real.
(calling out the door)
I'm shutting the door now! Sorry!
(He shuts the door.)

SLAKE

So you've told them.

JOSEPH
Oh yes. Right down to marketing. No secrets here. And the con-sensus is, play your cards right, you could get a book deal out of this.

That's assuming you've done this sort of thing before and are willing to tell all. Perhaps you're not. Anyway, no need for an answer now.

SLAKE

You're not worried?

JOSEPH

About . . .

SLAKE

Rumors.

McALVANE

You know how they spread.

JOSEPH

Heavens no! We're used to that in publishing. No, I'll tell you what I am. I am outraged and morally appalled by the both of you! How DARE you do this to me! Or to *anyone*? Is there some right you have that the rest of us don't know about? Some arcane inquisitional law? I don't think so. I mean who the fuck do you think you are?

McALVANE

(*with a cold grin*)
Don't you mean "whom"?

JOSEPH

Whom the fuck?
(*turns to* SLAKE)
I had no idea—you employ the *handicapped!* No, really, that speaks well for you. First thing that does.

McALVANE

Fuck you.

JOSEPH

Temper, temper!
(*to* SLAKE, *re himself, with a laugh*)
Look who's talking!
(*to* McALVANE)
Sorry. Let's forget this part. Can we be friends again?

MCALVANE

No.

JOSEPH

No, you're right, of course we can't. None of us will ever be what I'd call "friends," will we? So how long will this take?

SLAKE

Not long.

JOSEPH

Good. Oh by the way, I'm sure by now you've noticed that my lawyer isn't here. Are you surprised?

SLAKE

No.

JOSEPH

Really!

SLAKE

As I said, all we want is some information. I would assume you passed all that on to him, and he concurred.

JOSEPH

"No need for a lawyer!"

SLAKE

So why waste money?

JOSEPH

What *else* do you think he said?

SLAKE

"Call me when they leave?"

JOSEPH

Besides.

SLAKE

I give up.

JOSEPH

He said, "If at any point you feel even *remotely* uncomfortable—

SLAKE

"Just say stop."

JOSEPH

His very words!

SLAKE

And we stop.

JOSEPH

Just like that.

SLAKE

Just like that!

MCALVANE

Wouldn't have it any other way.

SLAKE

So then . . .
        (opens a notepad)
How often would you say you use your computer?

        (JOSEPH *stares at* SLAKE, *surprised.* SLAKE *and* MCALVANE
        stare back, expressionless.

        Lights up on ASTRAKHAN.)

ASTRAKHAN

How it's done . . .
        (beat)
Assuming your target's well protected—because where's the fucking
challenge if it's not?—what you look for is what we "in the business"
refer to, politely, as a backdoor, and, impolitely, bunghole.

It's no accident! The whole thing's highly sexual, it is, I'm erect almost the entire time. Really, breaking into where you're not supposed to go, it's a kickass fucking turn-on. And I do it . . .
(beat)
Because I can.

(*Lights back on* JOSEPH, *et al.*)

JOSEPH

My *computer*?

SLAKE

Yes. How often would you estimate that you use it in, oh, say, an average week?

JOSEPH

Just about every day.

MCALVANE

But not *every*.

JOSEPH

No. For example, today I probably won't touch it at all.

SLAKE

Then why's it on?

(JOSEPH *turns to look at his computer.*

Beat.

Lights back on ASTRAKHAN)

ASTRAKHAN

So what you look for are these entranceways.
(*Beat*)
And when you finally make it through there is such intense pleasure it's like electronic cum. It's the truth! Really, I keep expecting the screen to get all blotchy. I only tell the truth. That's because lying is obscene. My mom used to lie. Or rather, the woman I *thought* was

my mom. Astrakhan, Glenda, forty-three, dental hygienist and sometime prostitute, stomped to death by her former husband, a tapdancer with Tourette's Syndrome. Lucky thing they were not my *real* folks. I'd be all fucked up by now.

(Lights back up on JOSEPH, *et al.)*

JOSEPH
The computer's on because of e-mail.

SLAKE
E-mail!

JOSEPH
Yes. Except for that, I don't use it much at all. And even then . . .

McALVANE
What?

JOSEPH
Well, most of my business correspondence, I dictate. And if it's personal . . .

SLAKE
Don't tell me you write long-hand!

JOSEPH
Yes. In fact, I prefer it.

McALVANE
(to SLAKE)
He's just an old-fashioned fellow!

JOSEPH
That's why I publish books.

SLAKE
Like that big one over there?
*(*JOSEPH *looks at a book on a table.)*

JOSEPH

You mean the Mapplethorpe?

SLAKE

Yes.

MCALVANE

Are you proud of that?

JOSEPH

What?

SLAKE

That book.

MCALVANE

Proud that you published it?

SLAKE

I'll bet he is.

MCALVANE

Why else would he have it out?

JOSEPH

Would you like a copy of your own?

SLAKE

No. But thank you anyway.

JOSEPH

Why? Have you ever looked at it?

SLAKE

Yes, Mr. Elliot.

MCALVANE

We all have.

SLAKE

Had to.

McALVANE

Part of the job.

JOSEPH

So *this* is why you're here!

SLAKE

Not at all. No.

McALVANE

Not even close.

SLAKE

(to McALVANE: *a correction)*
Well . . .

McALVANE

(back to SLAKE*)*
It's *sort* of close.

(They turn to JOSEPH*)*

SLAKE and McALVANE:

(together, to JOSEPH*)*
It's *sort* of close.

(Lights back on ASTRAKHAN*)*

ASTRAKHAN

And you find these secret entrances because they were . . . *left*
there! Yes! Can you believe it? Not for you, oh no, but they might
as well have been. No, they've been left by the people who designed
the basic system, its security! Because every now and then they like
to go back in—*just to see what's doing.* It's like going home again.
Really! And you have to understand all that to be any good at this.

(Lights back on JOSEPH, *et al.)*

SLAKE

What about the Internet?

JOSEPH

The Internet?

SLAKE

Yes.

McALVANE

How often would you say you use the Internet?

JOSEPH

I would say, as little as possible.

SLAKE

Really!

JOSEPH

Yes. I find it mostly a great waster of valuable time. *Like both of you.*

McALVANE

Does that hold for weekends as well?

JOSEPH

Weekends?

SLAKE

Yes. How often would you say you use the Internet then?

(JOSEPH *stares back, puzzled.*

Lights back on ASTRAKHAN.)

ASTRAKHAN

And so you find this back way in because there are certain telltale signs experience has taught you to look out for, the equivalent of footprints, almost ghostly, an extra digit here and there, I mean sometimes that's all it is. And then, once you're in

. . . Well, you're like a mouse in the woodwork, just nestled there, quiet, watching, *waiting.*

(*Lights back on* JOSEPH, *et al.*)

JOSEPH

On weekends, I would say that if I can help it, I don't use the Internet at all.

SLAKE

And can you?

JOSEPH

What?

McALVANE

Help it.

JOSEPH

The computer is not something I find difficult to resist, especially on weekends, when I use it mostly as a paperweight. Sorry, but I just don't keep records of things like this. I don't "clock in."

SLAKE

But there are records kept.

JOSEPH

Well then check the fucking records!

SLAKE

We have.

JOSEPH

So then you know!

SLAKE

That you in fact use it all the time.

McALVANE

Five, six hours at a stretch.

SLAKE

Sometimes even more!

JOSEPH

I believe you have mistaken me for someone else.

SLAKE

I don't think so.

(*Beat.*

Lights back on ASTRAKHAN.)

ASTRAKHAN

So let's say, now you're "INSIDE THE SYSTEM"!

If you choose, you don't have to stay. You can leave a surrogate behind, sometimes called a "sniffer." That's because it—you guessed it!—sniffs. For *other* telltale signs. Like passwords. Passwords are the key. Because your target has a whole set of 'em, which he uses to go places he'd prefer you didn't know about.

And those passwords are what you want.

(*Lights back on* JOSEPH, *et al.*)

SLAKE

(*to* MCALVANE)

Mr. Elliot's memory seems to be failing him.

MCALVANE

(*reading from a notepad*)

Three weekends ago, both Saturday and Sunday, you were online almost all day and night. We have your log line, your phone records.

SLAKE

Does *that* ring a bell?

JOSEPH

. . . Actually, yes, that does.

SLAKE

Why were you online so much?

JOSEPH

I was online because I was trying to get help.

MCALVANE

About what?

JOSEPH

My computer. I had somehow screwed it up. I'm sorry: what exactly do you *think* I did?

SLAKE

(*to* MCALVANE)
Show him.

(MCALVANE *shows* JOSEPH *a sheet filled with data. As* JOSEPH *starts to examine it, lights come back up on* ASTRAKHAN)

ASTRAKHAN

And this "sniffer" senses when a password's been given, and instantly freezes the screen. "Sorry!" says the message. "Didn't catch that. Could you input your password one more time?" And so your unsuspecting target types in his password one more time. And this time you *capture* it! And with that, the system's yours. You are the owner now. Which is when the *real* fun begins.

(*Lights back on* JOSEPH, *et al.*)

JOSEPH

(*re the list*)
What the hell is this supposed to mean?

SLAKE

The time has come to stop pretending.

JOSEPH

I am not pretending!

MCALVANE

(sly grin)
Nor is your wife, it seems.

JOSEPH

My *wife*?

MCALVANE

Should I show him those as well?

SLAKE

No, let's just send the whole thing to his lawyer. I'm getting tired of
this man.

JOSEPH

What the fuck are you talking about!

MCALVANE

You don't have to go to jail for this, you know.

JOSEPH

I said what the hell are you—

SLAKE

We *heard* what you said!

MCALVANE

In fact, neither *one* of you needs to go to jail for this.

JOSEPH

Neither *one*?

SLAKE

Well, *she* might.

MCALVANE

Yes, sorry. *She* might.

SLAKE

Still, who knows, maybe not.

MCALVANE

Assuming you "cooperate."

(JOSEPH *pushes an intercom button.*)

JOSEPH

Could you get me my attorney, please?

(*They stare at him.*

Lights off on JOSEPH, *et al.*

Lights up on ASTRAKHAN.)

ASTRAKHAN

I did not set out to discover Joseph Elliot's secrets. My sole intention was to get into his renowned writing class, which he gave on Wednesday nights at the New School in New York, where I'd just arrived.

Lest you jump to any wrong conclusions, I should point out, my interest in his class had nothing to do with writing. I hate writing; always have. No, put simply, there was a girl enrolled in it whom I wanted very much to fuck.

That was before I saw Joseph's wife. *Met* his wife. *Fucked* his wife! Eight times! In three days, ten more in the next two months, once in their very own apartment, which I thought was a little risky, but she said no, let's do it here, on the pool table, and then there was the stain, but she said that doesn't matter, he won't notice it. Joseph doesn't notice things like that. Am I being indiscrete? I'm sorry but there's no avoiding it. Not if honesty is to be our policy. And truth to be told.

In that regard, I must add this: To get into Joseph's class, you had to submit a sample of your work. Not an unreasonable request! Unfortunately, I had nothing to submit. So I submitted someone else's—an unpublished piece, staggeringly obscene, written by a sex-crazed friend of mine who'd died of an overdose so, I mean, *he* wasn't going to know.

Mind you, I'm not proud of this. I simply tell you this so you may know the truth. It's important to be honest, I really do believe that, and, whenever possible, I am.

(*beat*)

Which means I probably should tell you this as well: though this particular event occurred almost five years ago, it so reshaped my life, not a day passes that I don't bring it back to mind, with, somehow, each time, some new detail emerging, until now it seems even clearer than it was back then. Funny, how memory works.

(Lights up on JOSEPH, *big smile)*

JOSEPH

Ah! Right on time! Come in.

ASTRAKHAN

Thank you, thank you.

*(*ASTRAKHAN *enters* JOSEPH's *apartment)*

JOSEPH

So nice of you to come.

ASTRAKHAN

No, please, so nice of you to have me—your house, your I mean apartment, this is such a beautiful place!

JOSEPH

Thank you.

ASTRAKHAN

Guess teaching must pay really well.

JOSEPH

. . . Ummm . . .

ASTRAKHAN

I mean, you know, in *general*. I ask 'cause frankly I'm still not altogether sure what direction I want my life to take and maybe teaching's something I should consider as a, you know, "backup"— just in case this fiction writing thing does not pan out.

JOSEPH
In general, teaching does not pay well.

ASTRAKHAN
So then this is all like, what, *inherited* money?

JOSEPH
Actually, I believe that's none of your business.

ASTRAKHAN
You know what? You are right. I should never have asked that, and I appreciate your honesty. Issue closed. That *street*! My God! What's it called again?

JOSEPH
Park Avenue.

ASTRAKHAN
Right, right. What a fuckin' street! When I publish my first novel, I tell you *this* is where I'm gonna live. I don't mean *here* of course, with . . .

JOSEPH
I understand.

ASTRAKHAN
You and your wife.

JOSEPH
I understand!

ASTRAKHAN
Nice as that might be!

JOSEPH
Right! No, I understand.

ASTRAKHAN
I just mean, you know . . .

JOSEPH

In the vicinity.

ASTRAKHAN

General vicinity. Exactly.

JOSEPH

Not a problem. So ... Would you like a drink?

ASTRAKHAN

Sure.
    (JOSEPH *heads for the bar*)
. . . Is she here?

JOSEPH

Who?

ASTRAKHAN

Your wife.

JOSEPH

Joanne?

ASTRAKHAN

Is that her name?

JOSEPH

Yes. Joanne. No, she'll be here soon. She works at Sotheby's and an
installation's going up that . . .
    (*off* ASTRAKHAN's *look*)
It's an auction house.
    (*again off his look*)
Art.

ASTRAKHAN

Ah.

JOSEPH
    (*heading back with drinks*)
You're not from New York, I take it.

ASTRAKHAN

No, California. Irvine.

JOSEPH

That's . . .

ASTRAKHAN

South of Los Angeles. Lot of airport noise. I'm sorry, should I take this off, or . . .

JOSEPH

Oh! Please! Of course!

ASTRAKHAN

I don't have a regular—you know, *sports* coat, jacket, just *this* which I actually even sleep in, so I didn't know if—

JOSEPH

No, no, you look fine, you're dressed fine. Here, I'll take mine off too.

(*They both take their jackets off.*

Pause.)

ASTRAKHAN

So you liked my story!

JOSEPH

Liked? No, if I had only liked it, you would not be in my class, or here tonight. I *loved* your story, Mr. Astrakhan. Have you been writing in this genre long?

ASTRAKHAN

Genre?

JOSEPH

Pornography.

ASTRAKHAN

Ah! No.

JOSEPH

No. Well, I mean, of *course* not—stupid question! How *could* you?
You're—what?

ASTRAKHAN

A student.

JOSEPH

No. Your age.

ASTRAKHAN

Fifteen.

JOSEPH

Fifteen!

ASTRAKHAN

I look older.

JOSEPH

I'll say! I mean, frankly, I'd have guessed, oh—

ASTRAKHAN

Eighteen, nineteen . . .

JOSEPH

Even twenty!

ASTRAKHAN

It's the drugs.

JOSEPH

Ah!

ASTRAKHAN

But! I don't do drugs anymore. Ask me why.

JOSEPH

Why?

ASTRAKHAN

Your class.

JOSEPH

My *class*?

ASTRAKHAN

Very first day, when that old lady read, the one you invited in—

JOSEPH

Grace Paley.

ASTRAKHAN

Her, yeah, I said, hey, your head has to be clear for shit like this, crystal clear—I don't mean crystal, I mean . . .

JOSEPH

I know.

ASTRAKHAN

No, crystal clear, I was right. My mind has got to be crystal clear for this, I said, or you are going under, *fast*! And ever since, I've been completely clean.

JOSEPH

Well that is wonderful.

ASTRAKHAN

It is. I'm very proud. So . . . You didn't think there was too much sex?

JOSEPH

Sex?

ASTRAKHAN

In my story.

JOSEPH
Ah! No, well, I mean, there was a lot! But then, the genre sort of demands that, doesn't it?

ASTRAKHAN
My English teacher thought there was too much.

JOSEPH
. . . Your . . .

ASTRAKHAN
High-school English teacher, she thought there was too much; *way* too much!

> (ASTRAKHAN *laughs at the memory.*
> JOSEPH *stares at him in shock.*)

JOSEPH
. . . I'm sorry . . . You showed that story to a high-school *English* teacher?

ASTRAKHAN
Had to. It was an assignment.

JOSEPH
An *assignment*?

ASTRAKHAN
And, by the way, I did not get a good grade.

JOSEPH
I'm not surprised.

ASTRAKHAN
In fact—actually?—they kicked me out of the fuckin' school over this. It's unbelievable! Especially when you consider that I was only doing what they asked.

JOSEPH
By any chance, do you remember how this assignment was worded?

ASTRAKHAN
Sure. "In ten pages or less, write about something significant that
happened to you during the past summer." Simple!

JOSEPH
Wait.

ASTRAKHAN
What?

JOSEPH
This *happened*?

ASTRAKHAN
What?

JOSEPH
This "story," what you describe in it . . .

ASTRAKHAN
You thought I made this UP?

JOSEPH
Of *course* I thought you made this up!

ASTRAKHAN
Wow.

JOSEPH
Mr. Astrakhan—

ASTRAKHAN
I'm like fuckin' tripping here.

JOSEPH
Mr. Astrakhan—

ASTRAKHAN
I mean obviously I can see why you might *think* I made this up. But
I can assure you everything I described happened exactly as I
described it.

JOSEPH

All the fucking.

ASTRAKHAN

All the fucking!

JOSEPH

Let me get this straight.

ASTRAKHAN

I fucked everyone.

JOSEPH

. . . In what sort of time frame?

ASTRAKHAN

I'd say about a week.

JOSEPH

A *week*?

ASTRAKHAN

Wild fuckin' week! Didn't get much sleep, I'll tell you! But, hey, fuckit, when you're fifteen—

JOSEPH

Why sleep?

ASTRAKHAN

Why sleep? And my teacher—I'm reading this in class—

JOSEPH

Aloud?

ASTRAKHAN

That's how we did it.

JOSEPH

To your English class.

ASTRAKHAN

Sophomore English class. I'm reading this aloud. And my teacher turns like purple. "Stop! Stop!" Talk about rude! I wasn't even through the first fuckin' sentence. So I said, shut the fuck up, this is our assignment, cunt!

JOSEPH

You didn't.

ASTRAKHAN

What?

JOSEPH

Say that.

ASTRAKHAN

Of course! I took homework very seriously. Or at least till this. "Stop! Stop!" So finally I stopped, because frankly I just couldn't take it anymore. "What I am reading here is the truth," I said. "Would you prefer it if I lied?" And she said—you won't fuckin' believe this, a certified high-school English teacher!—she said, get this: "Yes! You're just a sophomore. In the sophomore year, you LIE!"

So I said adios, cuntface, and out I went. Fuck school I said! Then I heard about the New School. And immediately came East. I mean this is something else. I'm like in heaven here. *Heaven*.

(JOSEPH *stares at him, speechless.*

Beat)

So how long do you think it'll take till I'm published?

JOSEPH

. . . *Published*?

ASTRAKHAN

One of the students said you were a publisher, too. You admire what I wrote; why not publish it?

JOSEPH

Well . . .

ASTRAKHAN

You don't publish porn!

JOSEPH

No . . .

ASTRAKHAN

You *do*?

JOSEPH

No, we don't publish individual, ummm ... *pieces*.

ASTRAKHAN

So . . .

JOSEPH

You need to write more.

ASTRAKHAN

Well this is very encouraging.

JOSEPH

Good.

ASTRAKHAN

Wow. My God. What you just said, what you just did? Believe it or not, that is the first piece of actual encouragement I have ever received. I mean that. I could fuckin' weep! If only someone like you had entered my life earlier, my life would be entire-
l
y
different now.

> (JOSEPH *stares at him.*
>
> ASTRAKHAN *stares back.*
>
> *Beat.*
>
> *Sound of a door opening. A moment later,* JOANNE *rushes in.*)

JOANNE

Sorry, couldn't get a cab, so I ran, I mean it. I'm drenched, through and through. Hi. I'm Joanne.

(*to* JOSEPH)
Is he the one?

JOSEPH

What?

JOANNE

Wrote that story.

JOSEPH

He's the one!

JOANNE

(*back to* ASTRAKHAN)
That story's positively filthy! And I loved every filthy word of it.

(*to* JOSEPH)
Tell him.

JOSEPH

She's a fan.

JOANNE

Even xeroxed it so I could show it around the office. My God! Who does your hair?

ASTRAKHAN

I do.

JOANNE

Not bad, not half-bad. Let me see your eyes.

(*She lifts his shades.*)
Jesus!

(*lowers them instantly*)
How *old* are you?

ASTRAKHAN

. . . Sixteen.

JOANNE

What the hell have you been doing?

JOSEPH

If you read his story, you know.

JOANNE

It's *true*?

JOSEPH

"Autobiography."

JOANNE

And you're still *standing*? Oh my God! Those shoes! Where'd you get those shoes?

ASTRAKHAN

Stole 'em.

JOANNE

Well steal me a pair!

JOSEPH

Joanne!

JOANNE

He's got style!
    (*to* JOSEPH)
How's the dinner?

JOSEPH

Done.

JOANNE

(*to* ASTRAKHAN, *re* JOSEPH)
The man's a miracle! Literary taste—and he cooks! Joseph doesn't invite just any old student here for dinner you know. You've been *honored*!

(*to* JOSEPH)
Start the clock. Five minutes, quick shower, out of these and I'm back. Go!

(*As she rushes off, calls*)
Wouldn't mind a martini!

(*Exit,* JOANNE.)

ASTRAKHAN

I don't think I've ever met anyone quite like her.

JOSEPH

Few have.

ASTRAKHAN

You're very lucky.

JOSEPH

Yes.

(JOANNE *returns, blouse almost off.*)

JOANNE

Change that to white wine.

JOSEPH

Gotcha.

JOANNE

(*to* ASTRAKHAN)
We must go shopping someday. *Love those shoes*!

(*Exit,* JOANNE, *undressing as she goes.* ASTRAKHAN *turns out.*)

ASTRAKHAN

(*to us*)
I remember him saying something about—I'm not sure, a writer I believe.

JOSEPH
(voice barely audible; distant; faint sense of an echo)
Have you read William Burroughs?

ASTRAKHAN
Burroughs, yes, but don't hold me to it, because at that point all I
could think about was her.
(to JOSEPH)
I think I'll go freshen up if that's all right.
(to us)
"Freshen up." I'd heard that in a movie somewhere, and it seemed
the right sort of thing to say.

JOSEPH
(distant sound, vague sense of an echo)
Of course. First door on the left.

ASTRAKHAN
(to JOSEPH)
Thank you. I'm so glad you invited me.
(to us)
And then I walked down the hall, *past* the first door on the left toward a
door at the far end that was slightly open. I could see a light. It was a bedroom. And I walked there. And pushed the door open the rest of the way.

*(A door opens revealing Joanne, in an odd light, completely
naked, her back to us, drying herself with a towel, but so
slowly it feels like a dream.)*

(to JOANNE)
Oh! I'm sorry.

*(She turns slowly, making no effort to cover herself with
the towel.)*

I have no idea how quickly she turned. I would suppose she turned
at a normal rate. But the moment has become so minutely defined
that it now seems timeless, and I can replay it at whatever speed I
choose, and yet know that it is right. That it is true.

(She stares at him, fully naked, still no attempt to cover up.)

JOANNE

The bathroom's at the other end.

ASTRAKHAN

End?

JOANNE

Of the hall.

ASTRAKHAN

Ah. Sorry. My mistake.

JOANNE

Not a problem. These things happen.

(As if by magic, "the door" shuts on her. And she is gone. ASTRAKHAN *turns back out.)*

ASTRAKHAN

When she came back out—maybe five minutes later, maybe ten—
she was in a light blue dress, loose fitting, delicate, and instantly I
knew—or *thought* I knew, no, felt *certain* that I knew, that she was
wearing nothing under it.

Whether that in fact was true or not, I could see in her eyes that
she realized that's what I was thinking. So in a sense it didn't really
matter if she was naked underneath. Because she might as well have
been, for that's how I saw her now. And she understood that. And
that is the truth of this moment, as I remember it.

*(*JOANNE *enters in a dress that, when lit a certain way,
shows her to be naked underneath. Which is how*
ASTRAKHAN *obviously sees her—though Joseph looks at her
as if she were perfectly clothed.)*

JOSEPH

Hi.

JOANNE

(eyes on ASTRAKHAN*)*

Hi.

JOSEPH

Feeling better?

JOANNE

Much.

(She walks up behind JOSEPH and puts her arms around
him, adoringly, and smiles past him—at ASTRAKHAN)

JOSEPH

Mr. Astrakhan was saying just now that I've changed his life.

JOANNE

How so?

ASTRAKHAN

He's given me a sense of purpose.

JOANNE

In what way?

ASTRAKHAN

Well, for example, the other day in class he quoted Flaubert.

JOANNE

Flaubert!

ASTRAKHAN

And I'd never heard of him.

JOANNE

Well then, you have a great deal of pleasure ahead of you.

JOSEPH

That's what I told him!

ASTRAKHAN

(eyes on JOANNE)
I hope you're right.

JOANNE

I'm sure of it.

ASTRAKHAN

Would you like to hear the quote?

JOSEPH

She knows it already.

JOANNE

He tells it to *all* his students.
(*with a smile*)
"Everything you invent is true."

(*lights off on everything but* ASTRAKHAN)

ASTRAKHAN

(*to us*)
It was in Chicago, at the Palmer House, that we fucked for the last
time. No warning! *Nothing!* Though I thought she did seem a little
distant as we went at it. But then, that could just be me, now, looking back. Can't be sure.

Anyway, when it was done—can't even conjure it, don't want
to!—she put on a robe, which was unusual; I mean, for her to cover
up—and then, said, straight out:

(*lights up on* JOANNE, *in a robe*)

JOANNE

That's it. No more. It is over.

ASTRAKHAN

Over?

JOANNE

Yes, love, over. I mean, what more can we possibly get out of this?

(*lights start to fade on* JOANNE)

ASTRAKHAN
(as the lights fade—an icy calm)
So then I ripped her robe off. "Stop!" she said. But of course I didn't.
Not till *I* was good and done. *"What more can we get out of this?"*
Showed *her* a thing or two. Yes, that scared her, I believe. Scared her
quite a lot. And she was right to be. *"No one does a thing like this to me!"*
    Then, I just *waited*.
    And of course *watched*. I love watching her . . .
    During which time—totally by accident!—I discovered what
Joseph's "secret" was.
    It's so fucking mysterious, isn't it? I mean the way paths some-
times cross, for no apparent reason, yet, when you look just a bit
more closely . . . Almost makes you believe there's a god.

*(A light—in the front hallway of the Elliots' apartment—is
switched on by* JOANNE, *who has just returned from work.
It is night. The rest of the apartment is dark.*

*From somewhere within, music can be heard, softly: the
first movement of Beethoven's Quartet, Op. 131.*

ASTRAKHAN *disappears from view.)*

JOANNE
. . . Joseph?

JOSEPH
(muted, flat)
In the living room.

*(She moves forward, startled that he's sitting in the dark,
and peers into the living room, where a dim light from
outside now reveals a shadowy unmoving form sitting in
a chair.*

She switches on a lamp.

*It's Joseph in the chair, staring out, expressionless, a bottle
of vodka and a glass on a table next to him. Also nearby: a
CD player, the source of the sound.*

She turns off the music.)

JOANNE

Joseph!

JOSEPH:

. . . Yes, dear. What?

JOANNE
(staring at him, startled)
What is it? What has happened?

JOSEPH
Well, believe it or not, I'm still actually not absolutely sure. But it would seem nothing good. In fact, it may well be catastrophic. Besides that, I'd say everything is fine! This chair is as it was, the floor is at it was, the front key still worked. And how was *your* day?

JOANNE
Why didn't you return any of my calls?

JOSEPH
Well, probably because I was at Larry's. I didn't go back to the office after that, just sort of walked around. Drink?

JOANNE

No.

(He goes to pour himself a drink.)

JOSEPH
(as he pours)
Oh, guess what I did at Larry's!

JOANNE

What?

JOSEPH
Threw up. No warning. Projectile vomit, I think they call it! Went halfway across the room! Splat! Right on the Aubusson! Never done a thing like that. Amazing feeling. Womp! Like a

cannon. Larry said not to worry. I like that in a lawyer. You sure you don't want a drink? I bet you do. You're just feeling shy.

(Pours her one. Hands it to her.)

Here's looking at you!

(He smiles, clinks her glass, then downs his drink in a gulp.

She just stares at him.)

JOANNE

Joseph . . .

JOSEPH

The funny thing is, it's not just me who doesn't understand how this has happened, Larry doesn't either. In fact, he says he's never come across anything quite like it—as if that would reassure me. Annals of law! I'll tell you what *did* reassure me. Him saying it's going to be all right. Wait! No. Sorry. That was his secretary. Said it to me on the way out! Guess I looked upset. Or maybe it was the shirt.

(She stares at his shirt, which is spotless.)

Oh, Larry sent out for a new one. That was nice of him, don't you think? Thoughtful! I told him to charge it to me, but he said no, no, it's on him. That gives you some idea of how bad things are.

JOANNE

How bad are they?

JOSEPH

Would you like the short version or the long? Actually, in this case, the long's not much longer than the short. So let's do that. You haven't touched your drink!

(To placate him, she takes a sip.)

Little more . . .

(She drinks down the rest.)

There we go!

(He refills her glass, speaking as he does.)

Well, the nearest I can figure, and Larry, too—assuming now that I'm innocent, which by the way Larry does believe! Or at least he says he does. No, I think he does. Pretty sure he does.

JOANNE

Innocent of what?

JOSEPH

Of the charges. Against you as well!

JOANNE

Me?

JOSEPH

Yes, you're in this. It's you an' me, babe. The fat lady's singing for us both! Anyway, nearest we can figure is that I made some sort of terrible blunder, inadvertently, three weekends ago, when you were up in Boston visiting—can't even remember now.

JOANNE

My mother.

JOSEPH

Oh yes! How is she?

JOANNE

Joseph.

JOSEPH

No, I mean it.

JOANNE

Doing fine.

JOSEPH

Really?

JOANNE

Yes, Joseph, really.

JOSEPH

I like your mother. She's got a lot of guts.

JOANNE
What did you mean by "blunder"?

JOSEPH
Ah! Well now. There it gets a little murky. I *thought* I was doing nothing of any consequence.
(heads for the bar)
How about a freshener?

JOANNE
Joseph!

JOSEPH
We have an author who has written a book called *Crisis*, filled with endless data on The Year 2000 Problem, and whose central thesis, in a nutshell says, head for the hills, Jack, it's all comin' down.

So I thought, if this author's right, there goes his book tour! In fact, everybody's book tour, to say nothing of everybody's salary, yours and mine included. On the other hand, if he's wrong, why are we publishing his book? You see what I mean?

So I said to myself, you'd best look into this! I was curious, nothing more. You were away. So out I went to the beach house—armed with this weighty tome and my new light-weight state-of-the-art portable computer, which I'd hardly used, but the author mentions all these supporting Web sites so I thought, I'll kill two birds with one stone—I'll read his book, and as I'm doing it, learn how to use my lovely new machine. It seemed an innocuous and foolproof plan.

So there I was, on the back deck, in a deck chair, pitcher of Bloody Marys by my side, mucking about on this new computer, which I was actually rather liking, merrily bopping from one Web site to another, all dedicated to The Year 2000 Problem, and each one by and large backing up our author's dire contention.

And you know what? I was persuaded. I was! Not because of all the data—We get book proposals every day proving that the world is flat, and with data, really, BUT!—because this crisis, even if it never happens, or happens just a little bit, is so . . . well . . . *beautiful*.

As a, you know, "Fuckup."

That's its category. "Avoidable Human Fuckups." I mean, it's like Mozart. Has that kind of perfection. So you just have to fucking admire it. Because it's fucking awesome! To fuck-up on a scale like that. I mean, it's the Parthenon of jokes. Who cares if it happens? What matters is, it *could*! What a way to end a century!

And suddenly it was as if veils were lifted, and I saw, with blazing clarity, that this exciting new global interconnected community we all live in now is just spit and polish, smoke and mirrors, it's a house of fucking cards, it is, and ready to come toppling at the slightest wind. And I thought . . .

What are their names, do you suppose? Those asshole computer whiz-kids who dreamed up that two-digit solution, all to save a little disk space? Because I'd like to sue them. I mean it. For substance abuse.

(She looks at him.)

Yes, dear. For they have abused us of our substance. We are nothing but abstractions now—strings of digits, signifying anything you want, floating in the ether.

And then I thought of Yeats. That pleased me! Always pleased when I think of him. And I thought, no, he had it wrong; that rough beast slouching toward Bethlehem isn't coming through a desert, it's coming through cyberspace, its monstrous body made entirely of zeroes and ones. The ceremony of innocence has been drowned, Joanne—in zeroes and ones.

(In the shadows, ASTRAKHAN stirs.)

So there I was, musing about the end of things, when all at once this message appears on my computer screen: "Possibly Fatal Error has occurred."

And I think, "Surely you exaggerate!"—and give the thing a little shove, whereupon the screen just sort of shrinks, amazing sight! as if Saran Wrap had squeezed everything together.

Which lasts only a moment. Bang!—it's back. Only this time it is telling me where I might FIND this "possibly fatal error"! It's trying to help! It's my FRIEND! Which I appreciate so much I believe I actually said thank you to the machine. I think I'm going to need another bottle.

JOANNE

I'll get you one.

JOSEPH

You're an angel.

JOANNE

So what did it say?

JOSEPH

"Possibly Fatal Error in partition 0001-CF-BX forward slash V"—or something like that. Anyway, I think, "Well this at least is helpful!"

(She brings a fresh bottle.)

And this is helpful too!

(As he talks, he opens the bottle.)

So I call IBM, because they *made* this fucking machine, and after about thirty minutes of waiting, a human voice is heard. And the fellow couldn't be nicer! "These things say fatal error all the time; they don't really mean it."

"Ah!" So he asks where the error is, in what particular partition, and I read him the information, and he says, "There is no such partition." So I say, "Well, I guess that's the fatal error." And he laughs and says yes, maybe so. I say, "So what do you think caused this?" He ponders for a moment, then says, "Gremlins prob'ly."

What's really scary is, he's not kidding. I mean he *is*; of course he is. But the fact is, he doesn't know what's gone wrong any more than I do.

But he does have a suspicion: which is that somehow I've done something wrong. I say, "I hope you don't mean with my *life*!" He says no, laughing, "With the computer. You've probably given it one too many commands. Or have a virus. Did you check for viruses?" "No." "Well, too late now. Do you have *another* computer around?"

"Yes, my wife's." "Well, use that one." And that's his advice.

So I hang up. And to my surprise, find I am in a state of seraphic bliss. Because, *because*, Joanne, at long last I know, and with a certainty that comes maybe once in a lifetime, know that I do not ultimately in any way shape or form NEED THIS FUCKING

COMPUTER! Fortified with this knowledge, I march inside and bring out *your* computer.

JOANNE

Didn't know I had one.

JOSEPH

Got it for you on your last birthday.

JOANNE

Oh yes . . .

JOSEPH

Working now swiftly but calmly, I mix up a fresh batch of Bloody Marys, bring out our second phone line, plug it into your "modem port"—

JOANNE

Without asking?

JOSEPH

Without asking. Yes. And *"access your modem."*

JOANNE
   (shivering with excitement)
My God!

JOSEPH

Which I found oddly stimulating.

JOANNE

I can imagine!

JOSEPH

Using *your* modem now, I call up our main phone line, to which my inert useless piece of shit is still connected, thinking maybe the gremlins inside will hear that tell-tale ring-a-ling and wake the fuck up.

JOANNE

Do they?

JOSEPH

Amazingly enough they do. And my machine comes alive!

JOANNE

You should have called Oliver Sacks.

JOSEPH

Good thing I didn't. Bad stuff is about to happen.

JOANNE

Your machine goes back into its coma.

JOSEPH

No, yours does.

JOANNE

My beloved little machine?

JOSEPH

Your beloved little machine.

JOANNE

Why?

JOSEPH

You are asking *me*? It shut down! "A Fatal Error has just occurred!"

JOANNE

What happened to "potentially?"

JOSEPH

Guess yours just took a more direct route.

JOANNE

Just from dialing *yours*?

JOSEPH

I think there may have been some kind of lethal feedback.

JOANNE

Are things like this supposed to happen?

JOSEPH

One assumes not. But for reasons humankind will never compre-hend, in this case it did. Zap. So I disconnected you. And got back to work on mine. Was I right?

JOANNE

To disconnect me?

JOSEPH

Yes. I figured you wouldn't want to just sort of, you know . . .

JOANNE

Linger there.

JOSEPH

Yes.

JOANNE

No, you did right.

JOSEPH

You'd do the same for me I'm sure.

JOANNE

Of course.

JOSEPH

It may come to that sooner than you think.

JOANNE

Joe!

JOSEPH

Somewhere in this next stage of my euphoria is when I suspect it must have happened.

JOANNE

What?

JOSEPH

According to this man in Larry's firm—Thompson, I think, *Jim?*
Yes! Anyway, he's their new computer guru, maven, on this Year
2000 Problem—they've set up a whole division! . . . Anyway, according to this guy, all it takes is one little slip-up and a hacker, if he
wants, can get into your machine, your system, and from there, do
anything you would do, if not more. Because once he has access to
your life, if he wants, he can *revise* it all.

This guy Thompson thinks, can't be sure, but *thinks* I must
have somewhere clicked on something or downloaded something I
shouldn't have. Which opened up a sort of door to my system, to my
files. And to my life.

And with this little door, whoever it was who'd been watching
me, and waiting—and he had to be, because clearly a lot of very
careful planning went into this—whoever it was, well, it was
enough for him.

And in he came.

And now it seems he has revised my life. No, rewritten it. I've
got a whole new history, Joanne. And it ain't a good one.

Nor is yours.

(She stares at him, scared.)

We think we know who it is. He's left a trail. Quite openly.
Apparently, he doesn't think he can be caught. He may be right.
Thompson says it's almost impossible to know where he actually is,
his messages are all time-delayed and routed in a Byzantine way
Thompson claims is like a work of art; I mean he's good at this. And
now—well, he's just sort of taunting us.

Which Thompson says in a way kind of helps, since it makes it
so clear that he's invented all of this. Or, anyway, . . . *most* of it.

The problem is: it all looks *real*, you see. Really does! In
fact, unless you're me, it's just about impossible to tell what's me and
what isn't.

He's made it look as if I'm engaged in child pornography.

JOANNE

Oh my God.

JOSEPH

And not just, you know, collecting it, but selling it. And on a massive scale.

JOANNE

But that's ridiculous!

JOSEPH

Of course, of course, but the evidence—if you want to *see* it as persuasive, is. I mean, there are receipts, Joanne, receipts from hotels I never went to, phone calls I never made, photos of me coming out of buildings I never visited. Sometimes . . . with children.

JOANNE

Joseph!

JOSEPH

The photos, Thompson says, can be done digitally. And the records—well, you just go back in and revise what was there, or add ones that weren't. He says it's not that hard if you know what you're doing. The FBI creates false identities all the time.

And while you're busy proving that it's false—which you may not be able to, not in every instance—it all leaks out. And the damage is done.

You're married to a child molester, dear.

And I'm married to a kind of porno star.

(*He picks up the packet* MCALVANE *had been holding, and which had been on the table next to him, takes out a photo, and hands it to her*)

JOANNE

Oh Jesus! Oh my God!

JOSEPH

That's Francis I believe. Standing on the side.

JOANNE

. . . Yes, but—

JOSEPH

I couldn't recognize the other two men.

(She drops the photo and runs out, holding her mouth.

He stares out.

In the distance, we can hear the vague sound of Joanne, retching.

He stares down at the picture she has dropped, picks it up and stares at it.

Joanne returns, ashen.)

JOANNE

That never happened, never, never, never!

JOSEPH

It's all right.

JOANNE

It is NOT all right! How the hell can you say this is all right?

JOSEPH

Well it does look like you.

JOANNE

Oh my God.

JOSEPH

So I was just saying that if it *were*—

JOANNE

But it's NOT!

JOSEPH

Can you be sure?

JOANNE

Can I be sure? Can I be fucking SURE?

JOSEPH
Because it really does look exactly like you.

JOANNE
Well it is NOT!

JOSEPH
And I believe you.

JOANNE
Really? Then why did you say just now are you sure? Did I ask you are you sure you didn't fuck a little kid or two along the way?

JOSEPH
Jesus.

JOANNE
No, I did not. I *trusted* you were telling me the truth! Trusted, Joseph! TRUSTED!

JOSEPH
And I trust you.

JOANNE
Well it didn't sound—Jesus! Oh my God. No . . .
        (She's just looked at the photo again)
This *is* me. This is, this is—fuck! oh fuck!—and this is Francis, this is him, it is, and this definitely is me in some I think hotel we went to, Monterey maybe, not sure, and I can even *sort* of remember him taking photos, but NO ONE ELSE WAS IN THE GODDAM ROOM! I'd remember that! *Fuck!* How'd they get hold of this?

JOSEPH
I wouldn't know.

JOANNE
Thank you for not saying you tell me.

JOSEPH
Francis could have left it somewhere, sold it, made a duplicate—

JOANNE

NO ONE ELSE WAS IN THE ROOM!

JOSEPH

Look, even if they were—

JOANNE

If they WERE?

JOSEPH

I am only saying—

JOANNE

I don't think I want to hear this.

JOSEPH

I am saying—

JOANNE

Joseph!

JOSEPH

I am SAYING! That even if they were, that is not the issue!

JOANNE

Not the ISSUE?

JOSEPH
(holding out another photo)
What about this one?

JOANNE

Oh my God!

JOSEPH
(weakly)
I find that one *particularly* disturbing since you have always . . .

(He stares at it too shaken to continue talking. For several moments, she can't speak either. Then finally, she says, barely audible . . .)

JOANNE

Who did this? Who is doing this to us?

(He sets the picture face down on the table, so he cannot see it, even inadvertently.)

JOSEPH

They believe a former student of mine.

JOANNE

Whom you fucked, I'm sure.

JOSEPH

Oh Jesus.

JOANNE

Probably can't even remember her name.

JOSEPH

Joanne!

JOANNE

Sorry, that's right, no, you said this was a man, I believe.

JOSEPH

Joanne!

JOANNE

Sorry! You were saying?

JOSEPH

. . . I was saying. . .

JOANNE

Francis happened *before* you, Joseph! Before, do you understand what that means? BEFORE!

JOSEPH

Of course I understand.

JOANNE

Do you really!

JOSEPH

Yes!

JOANNE

So then why don't I believe you?

JOSEPH

Look—

(*She grabs the two photos from the table and rips them into shreds.*)

JOANNE

(*icily calm*)
So now. You were saying. . .

JOSEPH

I don't know anymore.

JOANNE

This student's name.

JOSEPH

Oh yes. Astrakhan. Costa Astrakhan.

JOANNE

Never heard of him.

JOSEPH

Five years ago, we had him here for dinner.

JOANNE

By *himself?*

JOSEPH

No! No—no. With all my *other* students. My "annual bash."

JOANNE

Ah.

JOSEPH

Neon hair. Neon shoes . . .

JOANNE

. . . Wait-a-minute . . .

JOSEPH

Claimed he was sixteen.

JOANNE

The student you kicked out for plagiarism!

JOSEPH

Knew you'd get it.

JOANNE

Neon shoes . . .

JOSEPH

Funny, he remembers you vividly.

JOANNE

From one crowded party?

JOSEPH

According to him, that's where it all began.

JOANNE

What?

JOSEPH

The affair.

JOANNE

The *affair*!

JOSEPH

Which he refers to as "a fuckfest."

JOANNE

Joseph, this is Alice in Wonderland!

JOSEPH

So did you fuck him or not?

JOANNE

I'm going to assume that is a joke.

JOSEPH

He lists all the dates.

JOANNE

He came for dinner once, Joseph! ONCE! The place was jammed with students. I don't remember anyone even remotely matching his description, and except for maybe a "good-night, nice of you to come!" doubt I even spoke to him.

JOSEPH

Do you remember taking a shower that night?

JOANNE

Why, does he remember me *smelling*?

JOSEPH

No.

JOANNE

I take a shower before every party, Joseph. It's a long-standing habit.

JOSEPH

I mean *during* the party.

JOANNE

I would not think so.

JOSEPH

He says he saw you nude.

JOANNE

In the *shower*?

JOSEPH

No, our bedroom, toweling off afterwards. During which you apparently made no attempt to cover up. Which he took as a sign of encouragement.

JOANNE

Doesn't ring a bell.

JOSEPH

You'd remember a thing like that.

JOANNE

It's the sort of thing I generally remember. Joseph, have you lost your mind?

JOSEPH

I'm not sure. But it's a possibility.
  (long pause)
He also believes I'm his long-lost father.

JOANNE

What!

JOSEPH

Actually, it's even more astonishing that that. Because—*You won't believe this!*—until he met me—*Talk about Fate!*—he hadn't realized his father was lost!
  (off her look of incredulity)
Right! I mean, he's as surprised by this as I am.

JOANNE

Joseph, darling, you *have* lost your mind.

JOSEPH
But you'll be pleased to hear, you are not his mother.

JOANNE
Well I can't tell you how relieved I am! I mean here we were fucking our brains out—

JOSEPH
He thinks Annabel was his mother.

JOANNE
Oh Joseph—

JOSEPH
What's more, he has documents that seem to back it up.

JOANNE
That's absurd! How can there be documents?

JOSEPH
Somehow he got hold of some old medical records . . .

    (He stares off, shaken

    Silence.)

JOANNE
I don't understand.

JOSEPH
    (with difficulty)
In 1977, Annabel and I were in Paris when the first signs of the cancer came on. She was in her sixth month. And we decided to abort, because the chemotherapy . . .

JOANNE
Joseph, Joseph . . .

    (She goes toward him as if to hug him, but he pulls away.)

JOSEPH

What's so astonishing is that he somehow got into the files at the American Hospital in Paris, where the abortion was done, and *altered* them . . . so that it now seems Annabel in fact delivered a healthy little boy on that day. Whom we decided to put up for adoption. *My terrible dark secret!* So we could focus all our energy on her chemotherapy. At that point, my real history and the false link up, inextricably.

JOANNE

And he is that boy.

JOSEPH

But of course.

JOANNE

Well, he is bloody fucking insane!

JOSEPH

I don't think anyone is disputing that.

JOANNE

Then where's the problem?

JOSEPH

Where?

JOANNE

Yes, Joseph. If he is so obviously insane, surely all you need to do—

JOSEPH

Joanne, Joanne, there are post-office boxes scattered like signposts all around this country, all in my name, to which more child porno has been sent than anyone in the government has apparently ever seen. If that is not a problem, tell me what is.

JOANNE

It is not a problem because clearly he set it all up.

JOSEPH

But that I cannot prove.

JOANNE

Of course you can! Just sue the little fucker!

JOSEPH

How? Where is he?

JOANNE

I don't know. Hire a detective! Hire ten!

JOSEPH

With what?

JOANNE

With *what*?

JOSEPH

We have no money left.

JOANNE

Joseph, wake up. Wake up!

JOSEPH

It's evaporated!

JOANNE

Money does not evaporate. Stocks and bonds do not evaporate.

JOSEPH

That's true only if they are made of paper. Something you can hold.

JOANNE

We have back accounts, Joseph!

JOSEPH

No more.

JOANNE

Joseph . . .

JOSEPH

They've been closed.

JOANNE

Closed?

JOSEPH

Electronically. And our money transferred halfway to the fucking moon and left there to drift, in the ether, in the gloaming. I mean it's somewhere! No one's eaten it. It's just unobtainable, digitally speaking.

JOANNE

Did you call the bank?

JOSEPH

Of course I called the bank, our brokers, everyone! Larry had three lawyers on the phone all day. They're all baffled. It's just gone. Puff, the magic dragon. Ah, but not to worry. He says he'll take care of us.

JOANNE

Who?

JOSEPH

Astrakhan. "My son." It's really rather nice of him! After all these years, you'd think he'd be bitter.

JOANNE

It's . . .

JOSEPH

Yes, sort of unexpected.
   (pause)
   Larry thinks he must have had it all in place, the altered records, photos, everything, just waiting to move in, like Hitler's Panzer Division. One night is all it took. For the *anschluss*. And by next morning . . . well, we had been *annexed*.
   If I could just step back, I would admire it. Because what he's done of course is written a kind of novel. Only not in the old

fashioned linear one-sentence-follows-the-other sort of way, but, somehow, in all dimensions, simultaneously.

A novel built of zeroes and ones.

And we are its characters.

(She stares at him.)

JOANNE

. . .Can't Larry—

JOSEPH

What? Can't Larry what? What would you have him do? Tell me and I'll call. Because, believe me, he'd like to know as well.

JOANNE

Well I would think that . . . well, for a start . . . why not just explain all this to those two Federal agents?

JOSEPH

And what exactly would you explain?

JOANNE

That all of this is fake.

JOSEPH

But all of it is *not* fake.

(staring at her; coldly)

. . . Is it?

(She stares back.

Pause)

Speaking for myself, there are things he has found—about me—and which he's tucked in with all the really dreadful "invented" stuff—which is going to come out, and which you will see and will n   o   t I think be especially pleased to see. Nothing really vile, nothing criminal, but then again nothing anyone would be proud of. And for all of that I am very deeply sorry.And though I can't be sure, I would suspect a similar situation may hold for you.

(He stares at her, waiting.

She stares back in silence.

Pause.)

At Larry's suggestion, I have resigned from Random House, effective immediately.

JOANNE
Oh my God.

JOSEPH
Larry also thinks you will have to resign from Sotheby's. It's all going to come out, you see; once again, overnight—the credit card records, the phone records, all showing "where I've been." And then the photos. Of me fucking all the kids. Proving it.

And then of course there's you.

I'm afraid there are more photos. *Many* more. Even some video tapes. Some seem to be quite recent.

JOANNE
(barely audible)
Have you seen them?

JOSEPH
(barely audible)
Yes.

JOANNE
Well I can tell you right now—

JOSEPH
(just words—numb)
I'm sure it's not you.

JOANNE
Oh Jesus.

JOSEPH
Well what do you *want* me to say?

JOANNE
"I *know* it's not you!"

JOSEPH
(without conviction)
I know it's not you.

JOANNE
Could you try that again?

JOSEPH
Joanne . . .

JOANNE
Please? One more time?

JOSEPH
(trying hard, but still nowhere close to convincing)
Of *course* I know it's not you!

JOANNE
(flat)
Good.

JOSEPH
Joanne—

JOANNE
I said good. *Good*, Joseph! I'm glad you don't believe it's me. Can't tell you how much hearing you say that means to me right now . . .

(She stares at him.

He stares back.

She turns and stares out.

He continues to stare at her.

The lights change. ASTRAKHAN *enters the room. But they do not notice him.)*

ASTRAKHAN

Like any homecoming, it will be difficult at first. For all of us. So much to get used to! But we will.

In time.

And then . . .

Yes . . .

It will all be, once again, as I remember it.

(He reaches out and, with one arm around each, draws them towards him, gently, lovingly.)

And I will take care of them, forever and ever.

(lights fade)

curtain

NOTE

In Louisville, where Y2K received its premiere, the role of Joanne
was played by a British actress, and the following substitution
was made on Page 44 of the script. There are certain thematic
advantages to having Joanne "foreign," and if that is how the play is
performed, assuming her country of origin is England, this same
substitution should be made.

ASTRAKHAN
(flat; expressionless)
Joanne Summerhays, born Joanne Elizabeth Simpson, October
fifth nineteen sixty-one in a small town not far from the
University of Manchester, where her father taught moral philosophy at the University and her mother taught the flute.

In 1983 Joanne graduates from Oxford with a first in Art
History, and the next fall accepts a position at Sotheby's, in New
York, as an administrative assistant specializing in jade and Chinese
porcelain.

No further changes are necessary.